Tell me...

WHO LIVES IN SPACE?

...and more about the Universe

CHRYSALIS CHILDREN'S BOOKS

First published in the U.K. in 2003 by Chrysalis Children's Books,
an imprint of Chrysalis Books Group PLC,
The Chrysalis Building, Bramley Road,
London W10 6SP, U.K.

This edition distributed in the U.S. by Publishers Group West.

British Library Cataloguing in Publication Data for this book is available
from the British Library.

Every effort has been made to ensure that none of the recommended
websites in this book is linked to inappropriate material. However, due
to the nature of the Internet, the publishers regret that they cannot take
responsibility for future content of the websites.

Produced by Miles Kelly Publishing Ltd
Bardfield Centre, Great Bardfield, Essex CM7 4SL, U.K.

Editorial Director: Anne Marshall
Editor: Mark Darling
Copy Editor: Sarah Ridley
Indexer: Jane Parker
Proofreader: Hayley Kerr, Leon Gray
Americanizer: Tracey Kelly
Designer: Michelle Cannatella
Artwork Commissioning: Bethany Walker

Editorial Director, Chrysalis Children's Books: Honor Head
Senior Editor, Chrysalis Children's Books: Rasha Elsaeed

ISBN: 1 844580 57 1

Printed in Malaysia

Contents

Make-its

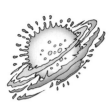

What's the biggest thing ever?

The Universe is bigger than everything else put together! It's so big that we can't use normal measurements to measure it. We use light years instead, meaning the distance light can travel in one year. If you used Earths as beads, it would take 742 million Earths to make a necklace one light year long. But if you think a light year is big, listen to this: the Universe is at least 12 billion light years across!

▼ *The Universe is foamy, like bubble bath—with galaxies as soap and bubbles of empty space.*

Universe

galaxy

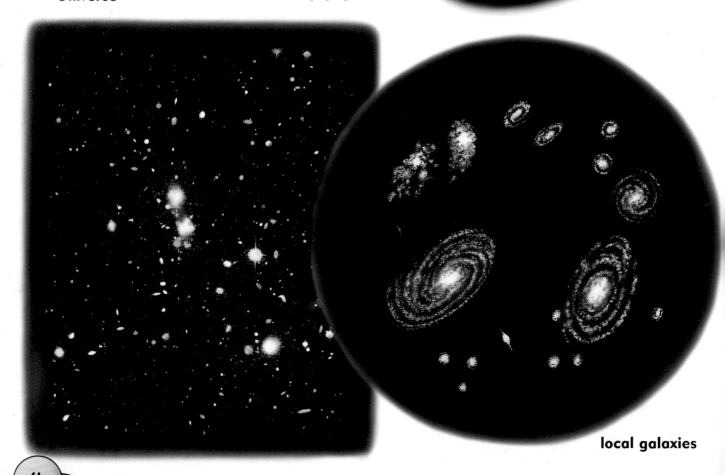

local galaxies

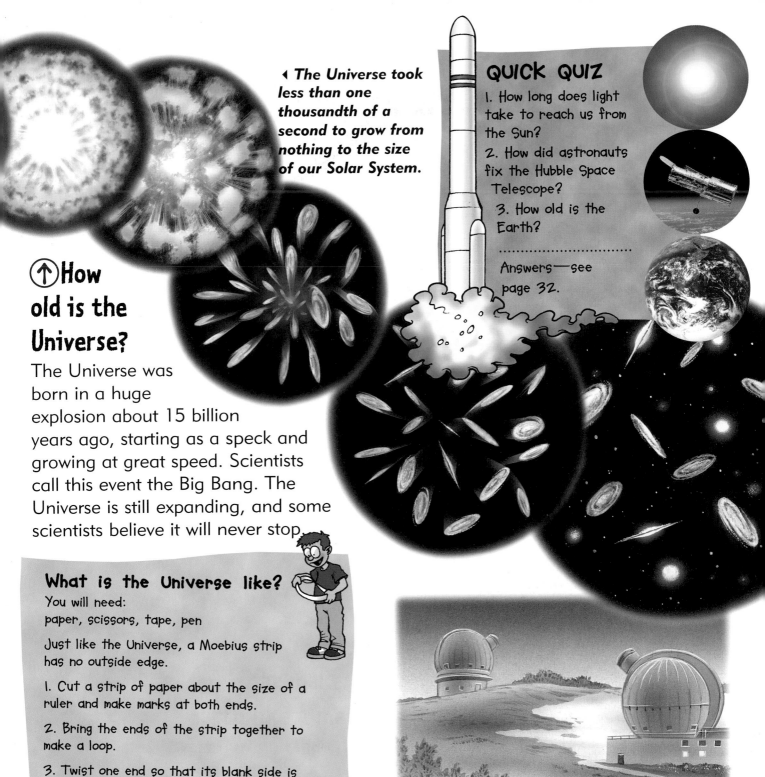

◄ The Universe took less than one thousandth of a second to grow from nothing to the size of our Solar System.

↑How old is the Universe?

The Universe was born in a huge explosion about 15 billion years ago, starting as a speck and growing at great speed. Scientists call this event the Big Bang. The Universe is still expanding, and some scientists believe it will never stop.

QUICK QUIZ

1. How long does light take to reach us from the Sun?
2. How did astronauts fix the Hubble Space Telescope?
3. How old is the Earth?

....
Answers—see page 32.

What is the Universe like?

You will need:
paper, scissors, tape, pen

Just like the Universe, a Moebius strip has no outside edge.

1. Cut a strip of paper about the size of a ruler and make marks at both ends.

2. Bring the ends of the strip together to make a loop.

3. Twist one end so that its blank side is connected to the marked side of the other end. Now tape the two ends!

Your piece of paper is now a Moebius strip. It has no outside edge! Try running a pen around it to see.

↑Where can I see the Universe?

Scientists called astronomers use telescopes to look far away into space. Some have huge telescopes in special buildings on top of mountains. But no one has a telescope that is powerful enough to see all of the Universe.

INTERNET LINK
NASA's resource for younger astronauts
http://starchild.gsfc.nasa.gov

 Do stars live in families?

On a clear night, you can see a cloudy stripe of light in the sky called the Milky Way. Although it looks like a cloud, it is actually millions and millions of stars. They are all part of the same family, or galaxy, of stars as our own Sun. All the stars in a galaxy swing around the heavy part in the middle where a black hole, which gobbles up nearby stars, may lurk. There are billions of galaxies in the Universe.

▼ *The Andromeda galaxy (M31) is the Milky Way's closest large neighbor, about two million light years away.*

INTERNET LINK
Build your own galaxy!
http://kids.msfc.nasa.gov/space/galaxies

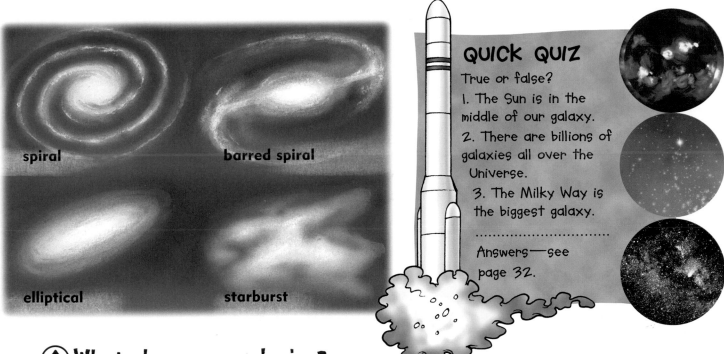

spiral

barred spiral

elliptical

starburst

QUICK QUIZ

True or false?

1. The Sun is in the middle of our galaxy.

2. There are billions of galaxies all over the Universe.

3. The Milky Way is the biggest galaxy.

....

Answers—see page 32.

↑ What shape are galaxies?

A lot of galaxies are like the Milky Way, a flat disk with a bulging middle. They look like two fried eggs glued back-to-back. Some have swirls and spirals, others are just big clumps of stars. Galaxies begin as small separate blobs, or starbursts. They fall together in spirals, which end up as big blobs, or elliptical galaxies.

↓ Do galaxies bump together?

Galaxies can run into each other, but they don't seem to notice! Stars in galaxies are so far apart that galaxies can pass straight through each other, like smoke passing through steam. Collisions can however change galaxies. The Cartwheel Galaxy, as seen below, rippled outward after the nearby smaller galaxy passed right through it.

Galaxy quest

- Scientists only discovered other galaxies within the last hundred years.
- The Andromeda Galaxy is rushing toward us at a speed of 190 miles a second!
- Black holes can swallow up other stars.
- Every patch of night sky hides thousands of galaxies!

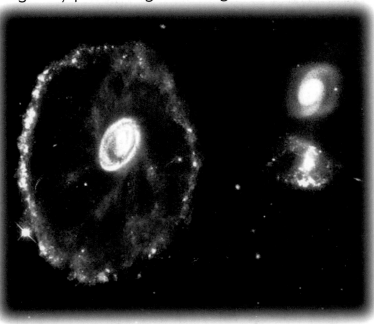

What makes stars shine?

Stars slowly burn themselves up in a raging fire, giving out light from the fire. The fire is driven by nuclear reactions deep below the surface, where atoms break down and release their energy. Stars range from between 2,800°C to 28,000°C at the surface, but can be thousands of times hotter at their core, or centre. They only seem to blink and twinkle to us because their light wobbles as it passes through Earth's atmosphere.

Hot spots

- Our star, the Sun, burns four million tons of fuel every second.
- Our Sun is actually very small. Red giants can be up to 500 times bigger.
- The small star Sirius B orbits Sirius once every 50 years.

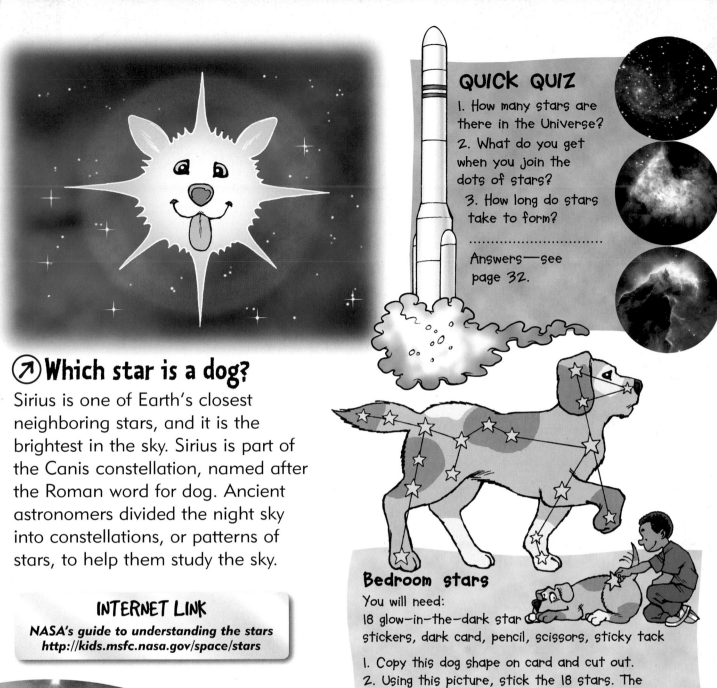

Answers—see
page 32.

QUICK QUIZ

1. How many stars are there in the Universe?
2. What do you get when you join the dots of stars?
3. How long do stars take to form?

⤢ Which star is a dog?

Sirius is one of Earth's closest neighboring stars, and it is the brightest in the sky. Sirius is part of the Canis constellation, named after the Roman word for dog. Ancient astronomers divided the night sky into constellations, or patterns of stars, to help them study the sky.

INTERNET LINK

NASA's guide to understanding the stars
http://kids.msfc.nasa.gov/space/stars

Bedroom stars

You will need:
18 glow-in-the-dark star stickers, dark card, pencil, scissors, sticky tack

1. Copy this dog shape on card and cut out.
2. Using this picture, stick the 18 stars. The constellation you have made is called the Greater Dog, and the star shining on the dog's chest is the Dog Star—the brightest star in our night sky. Stick your constellation high on your bedroom wall—and see the stars shine just after you turn the lights out!

← Where do stars come from?

Stars are born out of space dust and gases that hover in a monster cloud called a nebula. Currents in the cloud cause some parts to become heavier than others, dragging more and more dust and gas toward them. When they form a big heavy ball, they begin to glow.

Do stars live forever?

Stars do grow old and die. For most of its life, the average star is small and yellow like the Sun. As its fuel runs out, it stops being heavy enough to hold down the hot gases at its surface, and it begins to fall apart. A layer of hot gas drifts outward in a giant cloud, and the core collapses to a hot cinder. The Sun is about halfway through its life span.

2 the lumpier pieces clump together to form a star

1 dust and gas form a cloud in space

5 the star blows apart and dies

3 a yellow, burning star, like our Sun

4 the star grows hotter and bigger, becoming a red giant

⬉ Which stars blow up?

Giant stars end their lives with a bang! When they begin to collapse, such huge energy builds up that it is all released in a giant explosion called a supernova. The explosion blasts dust and gas from the dead star across huge distances.

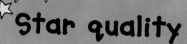
⬇ Which star sounds like an alien?

Some stars act strangely after they die. Their core collapses to become a pulsar, spinning up to a thousand times a second and sending out radio waves. The first one to be found by a radio scientist was called LGM, or Little Green Man, because its radio pulses looked like alien morse code! We use special radio telescopes to listen in.

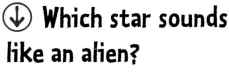

black hole

⬈ Which stars become invisible?

The weirdest stars of all stop glowing and start eating the light around them. They become so heavy that light rays are caught in the grip of their gravity and fall in, making them seem completely black. They are called black holes. There may be a big one at the center of our galaxy.

INTERNET LINK
Questions and answers about the Universe
http://scifiles.larc.nasa.gov/treehouse.html

Which planets are our neighbors?

Earth's sister planets are Mercury, Venus, and Mars, named after Roman gods. They are all rocky planets close to the Sun. Mars is further away from the Sun than Earth and has less atmosphere. It is enough like Earth for many people to think we could adapt it to make a second home in the Solar System. Mercury and Venus are much closer to the Sun, and both are blasted by the Sun's intense heat.

▼ *From left to right, Mercury is closest to the Sun and Pluto is furthest away.*

INTERNET LINK
More about astronomy and telescopes
www.dustbunny.com/afk

Jupiter

Mars

Earth

Venus

Mercury

Sun

⬿ Do planets glow in the dark?

No planet has its own light source, except manmade ones on Earth. We only see planets because light from the Sun bounces off them. The reflection is too weak to see in daytime, but when the Sun is hidden beyond the horizon, the glow is visible. Venus is the easiest planet to see. Look for it where the Sun has just set, or where it's about to rise in the morning. It looks like a bright star.

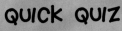

⬿ Can I fly around the Solar System?

If you had a spacecraft as fast as a jumbo jet, it would take you around 1,500 years to fly from one side to the other. But why bother? The Earth whirls you around the interesting part of the Solar System once each year at 67,000 miles an hour!

Saturn

Uranus

Neptune

Pluto

Make our Solar System

You will need:
card, pencil, pens or crayons, thread, coat hanger

1. On card, draw the Sun and all nine planets. You can copy the main picture on this page if you want.

2. Cut them out and color them.

3. Tape a piece of thread to each one. Taking an old wire coat hanger, tie each planet to the hanger, starting with the Sun and going out in order to Pluto.

Now watch those planets spin in the breeze.

Why is our planet full of life?

Earth is the only place where we are sure that life exists. Until we find life elsewhere, it's hard for scientists to say what it is about Earth that makes it perfect for life. Part of the reason may be that the Earth is the right temperature for liquid water, and that it is covered by a protective blanket of gases. This blanket is called the atmosphere—it carries water all around the world as clouds.

▶ *Earth's atmosphere is made up of different layers of air.*

thermosphere
53 miles upwards

aurora

mesosphere
31–53 miles

meteor shower

stratosphere
9–31 miles

maximum height for a balloon

troposphere
up to 9 miles

Mount Everest

maximum height for an airplane

clouds

⤵ Is the Earth round like a ball?

People used to think the Earth was flat like a pancake, because that's how it looks if you're standing on it. But then the Greeks realized it was ball-shaped by carefully measuring shadows. Modern science can tell it's not quite a perfect ball—the Earth bulges a little in the middle, around the Equator.

QUICK QUIZ

1. Earth's atmosphere is less than 1% carbon dioxide: true or false?
2. When did Earth's last cold snap, the Little Ice Age, peak?
3. What percentage of the Earth's surface is dry land?

....

Answers—see page 32.

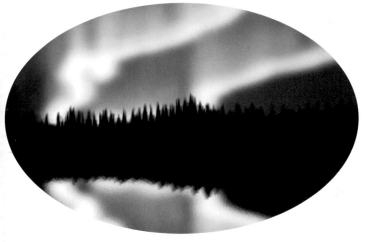

▲ *At the poles, the Earth's magnetic field can cause amazing fireworks in the sky, called the aurora.*

⤵ How is our planet in a spin?

Like most things in the Solar System, Earth doesn't just circle around the Sun. It also spins like a basketball balanced on one finger. That's why you're in daylight for half the time and pointing away from the Sun for the other half. It takes 23 hours, 56 minutes, and 4 seconds for Earth to spin around once on its axis. The Earth also moves through the Milky Way with the rest of the Solar System.

Down to Earth

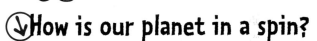

- Earth is like a peach, with a skin (land and sea), a mushy part (molten rock), and a big seed in the middle.
- A huge magnetic field protects the Earth from solar winds.
- Space starts around 62 miles above your head.
- The scientific name for Earth is Terra.

INTERNET LINK
Everything you need to know about Earth
www.nasm.si.edu/ceps/etp/earth

Are there seas on the Moon?

There are 30 seas on the Moon, but not a drop of water! They are actually large, dry plains of dark volcanic rock. To early astronomers, the patterns they create looked similar to the maps of Earth's oceans. An Italian astronomer called Riccioli decided to name these areas seas in 1651. He made up beautiful names, such as Sea of Tranquillity and Sea of Nectar. From Earth, the Moon seems to be changing shape all the time. These shapes are called the phases of the Moon.

← Which planet has the most moons?

Saturn has at least 31 moons, but may have more! It's hard to tell, because many of the smaller moons stay close to Saturn's amazing rings, a bright belt of ice crystals that stretches all around the planet's equator.

▼ *You won't see all these features with the naked eye, but sometimes if you squint, you may see a face!*

Yummy Moon craters

You will need:
2 egg whites, 1 1/2 cups shredded coconut, 3/4 cup caster sugar, 2 teaspoons cornflour

1. Ask an adult to preheat the oven to 325°F.

2. Beat two egg whites in a bowl until they're stiff. Add 1 1/2 cups shredded coconut, 3/4 cup caster sugar, and two teaspoons of cornflour.

3. Shape the dough into 12 crater-shaped mounds and place on a cookie sheet that you've lined with a piece of rice paper. Ask an adult to bake the moon craters for 20 minutes.

4. Cool moon craters on a wire tray before eating.

Dive in—they're out of this world!

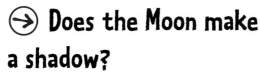

➔ Does the Moon make a shadow?

The Moon is only about as wide as Australia, but that's big enough to cast quite a shadow. When the Moon passes directly between the Earth and the Sun, it casts a shadow up to 168 miles wide on the Earth, with a dark spot in the middle that is about 2 miles across. This is called a solar eclipse.

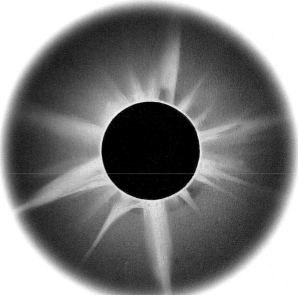

↙ Which moon might have life?

The *Galileo* space probe took some very interesting closeup photos of one of Jupiter's moons, Europa. The moon appears to be covered in ice that behaves as though it covers an ocean world. If there's liquid water on Europa, there could be life, too.

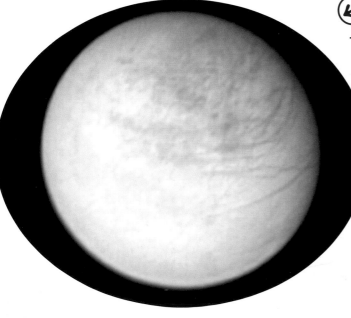

INTERNET LINK
Masses of Moon facts
www.stemnet.nf.ca/CITE/solar_sys_moons.htm

Which planet's a fast mover?

The little planet closest to the Sun whirls around, taking just 88 Earth days to complete a full circuit of the Sun. That's why Mercury is named after the messenger of the Roman gods. It is scorched by the Sun on its daylight side and freezing cold on the night side, because it has no protective atmosphere. Mercury spins so slowly that its days last longer than its years.

◄ *The surface of Mercury looks almost identical to our Moon.*

Close to home

- The air at ground level on Mars is about as thin as it is 22 miles above the Earth.
- Venus spins backward, just like Uranus and Pluto!
- Fragments chipped from Mars by meteorites have landed on Earth.
- The science of changing Mars to be more like Earth is called terraforming.

↙ Which planet's a real scorcher?

Venus, our nearest neighbor, is cloaked in white clouds, making it glow brightly in the sky. But Venus suffers from a terrible greenhouse effect, with a carbon dioxide atmosphere and sulfuric acid clouds. At ground level, temperatures are constant at 480°C—if rain was to fall, it would be boiling acid. Ouch!

QUICK QUIZ

1. Is Mars bigger than Earth?

2. Have aliens carved canals on the surface of Mars?

3. Mars' biggest moon is only 16 miles across: true or false?

....

Answers – see page 32.

Answers – see page 32.

↓ Is Mars flat or hilly?

Mars has some very boring plains and a large, flat basin around its north pole that looks like it was once the bottom of a shallow sea. But it also has what might be the largest volcano in the whole Solar System. Olympus Mons is 13 miles tall and 375 miles wide! There are also huge canyons and mountains.

↖ Which planet's turned rusty?

Mars is also called the red planet, and was named after the Roman god of war because of its bloody appearance. The redness is caused by rust. Martian soil is rich in iron, which has oxidized (reacted with oxygen) to form rusty powder. It covers the land and is blown around in giant dust storms.

Can we visit the gas giants?

Most of the lighter, gassier material in the cloud that created the Solar System stayed much further out from the Sun than the rocky planets. The closest of the gas giants, Jupiter, is about eight times as far from Earth as Mars. Until we invent a quicker type of spaceship, the best way to visit the gas giants is by sending a probe. The Voyager probes passed by in the 1970s. They scanned the surface of the planet and beamed data home from their big transmitters. The data was used to print beautiful photographs of the planet.

▸ *Probes don't carry human passengers, so they don't have to come back to Earth.*

INTERNET LINK
Meet the Saturn probe, Cassini
http://eis.jpl.nasa.gov/~skientz/cassini

← Where's the scariest storm?

Jupiter is a stormy planet, but one storm stands out—the Great Red Spot. It has been howling for at least 300 years. It is an amazing 8,700 miles wide and at least 25,000 miles long. That's a hurricane as big as three Earths, and it never stops howling!

Biggest and best

- Saturn isn't the only planet with rings—Jupiter, Uranus, and Neptune also have small rings.
- Jupiter radiates more heat from its hot core than it collects from the Sun.
- As pressure increases further down in Jupiter's atmosphere, the gas gradually turns to liquid.
- Jupiter weighs twice as much as all the other planets put together.

↑ Which planet wears rings?

Saturn has a huge belt of ice crystals orbiting its equator like the brim of a hat. The rings may be the remains of broken-up moons. Although the largest ring visible from Earth is about 170,000 miles across, it is only 320 feet thick.

Which planet came as a big surprise?

Most planets in the Solar System were known about before the telescope, so no one expected to discover a whole new planet. Around 200 years ago, an astronomer named William Herschel spotted something moving out there. At first he thought he might have discovered a comet, but it turned out to be a planet about 15 times heavier than Earth! Uranus lies far beyond the visible gas giants, about as far away again as the distance to Saturn.

▲ **William Herschel was the first astronomer to study beyond the Solar System, and he discovered thousands of star systems.**

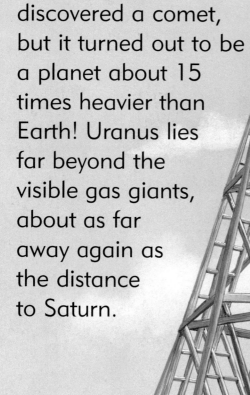

◄ **After discovering Uranus, Herschel built his famous telescope, which was bigger than a house!**

→ Which world is the windiest?

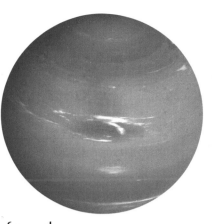

The distant planet Neptune is dark, but it's certainly not dull. The *Voyager 2* probe found that Neptune had a storm system to rival Jupiter's Great Red Spot. It was nicknamed the Great Dark Spot—wind speeds are around 1,200 miles an hour!

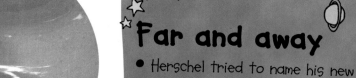

Far and away

- Herschel tried to name his new planet after the British monarch, King George III.
- Uranus is the only planet with poles that point at the Sun—the South Pole for 42 years of the orbit, and the North Pole for the other 42 years.
- Neptune is 2.8 billion miles from the Sun.

← Which world is most far-out?

Pluto loops farthest away from the Sun, but sometimes its oval orbit takes it inside the orbit of Neptune. Pluto is smaller than Triton, Neptune's largest moon, and some people think that both Triton and Pluto were wandering loose until Neptune grabbed Triton.

↑ Is it colder away from the Sun?

Planets farther from the Sun receive much less energy, just as your hands get less warmth as you move them away from a radiator. Neptune makes its own heat, but it's still −210°C at the top of the clouds. On Pluto, scientists believe that gases such as methane and nitrogen are deep-frozen on the surface.

Make yourself a Pioneer space plaque
You will need:
glue, gold foil, card, pen lid

1. Glue some gold foil on a rectangle of card—be very careful because foil can easily tear.

2. Engrave the picture shown here—a pen lid makes a good tool.

This is the plaque that was attached to the Pioneer space probes, made from aluminum and covered with gold to withstand the fierce heat in space. The plaque shows a man and a woman, and a map of how to find Earth—just in case any friendly aliens felt like visiting!

INTERNET LINK
Beautiful outer planet pictures and info
http://photojournal.jpl.nasa.gov

How can a belt be made of rock?

The big gap between Mars and Jupiter contains a loose belt of boulders and rocks called asteroids. The asteroid belt is more heavily populated in some parts of the orbit than others. The biggest asteroid is about 600 miles across, and some are no bigger than a small car.

▲ Some scientists think that the dinosaurs died out after a big asteroid smashed into the Earth.

▲ Asteroids may be rocks that never fell together to make a planet.

INTERNET LINK
A great site for comet fans
www.learnwhatsup.com/astro

↘ Why do comets have tails?

Comets are made of dust, rock fragments, and frozen water, like a dirty snowball. As they drop in toward the Sun from the outer edges of the Solar System, they begin to boil, leaving a trail like a steam train. Some have two tails. One tail is made by the comet's trail of dust. The other is formed by gas particles, which are blown in a straight line away from the Sun by the solar wind. People used to think comets were bad luck.

QUICK QUIZ

1. How often is Halley's Comet visible from Earth?
2. How big is the average shooting star?
3. Which meteor shower delivered more than 46,000 meteors in less than half an hour?

....
Answers—see page 32.

☆ Space trash

- Some meteors don't burn up completely—ones that hit the ground are called meteorites.
- A few thousand tiny meteorites land on Earth each year.
- A meteorite strike in Siberia, Russia, in 1908 was so loud the noise knocked people off their feet.
- In 1910, the Earth passed through the tail of Halley's Comet, causing panic but no damage.

↙ When does the sky rain stars?

Small fragments from comets and tiny asteroids sometimes cross Earth's path around the Sun, and are swept up in our atmosphere. Because they are traveling at high speed, they heat up and create a streak of light in the sky, called a meteor or shooting star, before finally burning up.

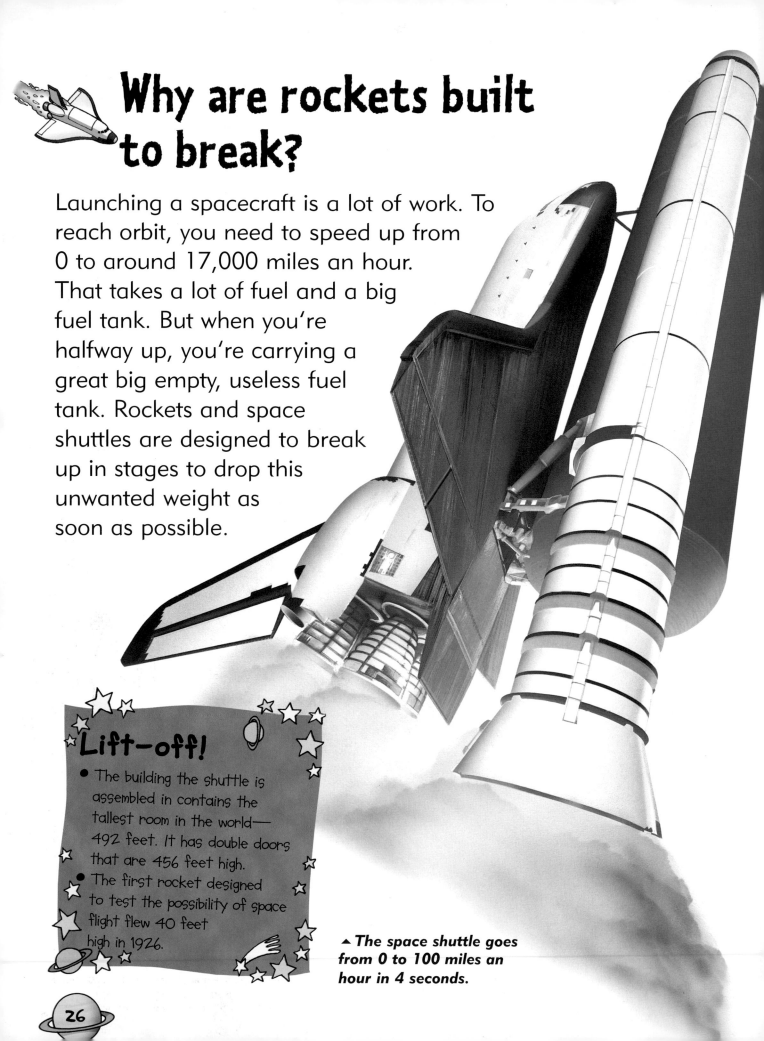

Why are rockets built to break?

Launching a spacecraft is a lot of work. To reach orbit, you need to speed up from 0 to around 17,000 miles an hour. That takes a lot of fuel and a big fuel tank. But when you're halfway up, you're carrying a great big empty, useless fuel tank. Rockets and space shuttles are designed to break up in stages to drop this unwanted weight as soon as possible.

Lift-off!

- The building the shuttle is assembled in contains the tallest room in the world— 492 feet. It has double doors that are 456 feet high.
- The first rocket designed to test the possibility of space flight flew 40 feet high in 1926.

▲ *The space shuttle goes from 0 to 100 miles an hour in 4 seconds.*

Which was the tallest rocket ever made?

The rockets that powered the Apollo Moon missions into deep space were the American Saturn rockets. *Saturn 5* was 364 feet tall, burned 14 tons of fuel a second, and reached a top speed of 25,000 miles an hour. Apart from the tiny crew module at its nose, the rocket was just three stages (with 11 engines) and fuel tanks.

How do shuttles land without a bang?

Shuttles don't so much fly as belly-flop back to Earth. They use the friction of the Earth's atmosphere to slow them down to gliding speed, and then glide very heavily back towards their runway. They have no engine to power a second attempt if they miss, so the runway is a long one—3 miles in fact!

Which rocket has wings?

The space shuttle was the first rocket designed to be recycled. There are three stages—the shuttle itself, with wings for gliding back to Earth; a huge fuel tank, which is cast off in space and burns up like a shooting star; and two long, thin, solid-fuel booster rockets, which are used up quickly and parachute into the sea.

fuel tank

booster rocket

shuttle

INTERNET LINK
Why do students want to travel into space?
www.seds.org

Who went for a spin on the Moon?

Apollo 15 astronauts took a Moon buggy with them to zoom around on the Moon. David Scott and James Irwin drove the battery-powered lunar roving vehicle for about 17 miles. The buggy had a top speed of 11 miles an hour.

INTERNET LINK
Fun space exploration site
www.artyastro.com

▶ **The Apollo 15 mission used a lunar rover to explore far more of the Moon's surface than had been possible on any of the previous Moon landings.**

⬅ Who first made footprints on the Moon?

The first man to walk on the Moon was Neil Armstrong, who stepped out of the *Apollo 11* lunar module in July, 1969. He was followed 15 minutes later by Buzz Aldrin (seen here). The two men spent 2½ hours collecting samples, and raised an American flag. They blasted back into space the next day, leaving behind a plaque commemorating the event.

⬇ Did animals go to space?

All sorts of animals have gone where man was too careful to go before. The first earthling in space was Laika, a Russian dog. Other animals were used to test that space was safe—some tortoises went round the Moon before any humans had been there.

One giant leap

- Valentina Tereshkova became the first woman in space in June, 1963.
- Voyager 2, launched in 1977, has gone beyond Pluto's orbit.
- No one has been to the Moon since December, 1972.
- Buzz Aldrin was the first human ever to go to the bathroom on another world.

⬊ Who was the first human in space?

The Russian Yuri Gagarin became the first human being in space in April, 1961. He completed a loop of the Earth in his *Vostok* space capsule in about an hour, before returning to Earth using a parachute.

Who lives in space?

Astronauts in the space shuttle are helping to develop the first international space station (ISS). Scientists from many countries can use the space station to live in and conduct science experiments. No one lives permanently in space. If you stay in weightlessness for too long, you lose some muscle strength and bone structure, so space-station staff have to exercise a lot. The record is held by a *Mir* scientist who spent 437 days in orbit.

▲ *The ISS is built from clip-together pieces brought by the space shuttle.*

▶ *Astronauts use a strap-on spaceship called an MMU to get around in space.*

INTERNET LINK
Start here for space-related questions
http://quest.arc.nasa.gov

▲ *Astronauts train to move big objects around in space and try out their suits in special training pools.*

QUICK QUIZ

1. How long was the longest spacewalk?
2. Will your bones break after a year in space?
3. Spacesuit helmets have special nose pincers so astronauts can unpop their ears: true or false?

....

Answers—see page 32.

⊙ Can astronauts take their suits off?

No one takes their suit off in space unless they are inside a spacecraft or space station. The vacuum of space has some gory effects on human bodies, including making the blood boil. In space stations and on the shuttle, the environment is controlled so that humans can live there safely.

Home from home

- Sleeping bags on the shuttle are attached to the wall to stop astronauts from drifting away.
- Instead of showers, astronauts on the shuttle use wet wipes.
- Dennis Tito, a US businessman, became the first space tourist in 2001. He paid $22 million.
- In weightlessness, your spine relaxes and you get taller – by 1–2 inches.

⊙ Do astronauts get travel sick?

Weightlessness feels like a roller-coaster, as you drop down a huge slope. It can make you feel sick, which is dangerous, because liquids can fly in all directions and mess up electronic equipment. So astronauts train on the world's most extreme roller-coaster, a jet plane nicknamed the vomit comet.

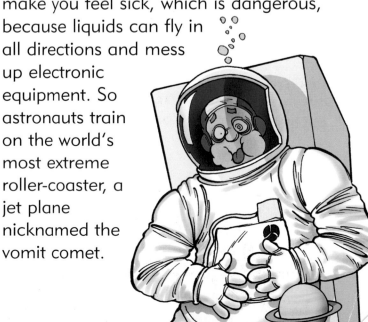

Index

Quick Quiz answers

Page 5
1. 8 minutes
2. They gave it mirrors
3. About 4.5 billion years

Page 7
1. False
2. True
3. False

Page 9
1. Ten billion trillion
2. A constellation
3. Millions of years

Page 13
1. Over 100 times bigger
2. Not yet, no
3. Yes

Page 15
1. True
2. 1750
3. About 30%

Page 19
1. No
2. No
3. True

Page 21
1. Europa
2. 21 pieces of a broken comet
3. Ganymede

Page 25
1. Every 76 years
2. About 2 millimetres across
3. The Leonids, November 17, 1966, Arizona

Page 31
1. 8 hours, 56 minutes
2. No
3. True